#RELATIONSHIPGOALS

AN INTERACTIVE COUPLE'S GUIDE TO DEVELOPING & MAINTAINING A RELATIONSHIP THAT IS DOPE IN REAL LIFE AND NOT JUST ON SOCIAL MEDIA.

BY JENNIFER ALLEN

We live in the day and age where #GOALS are everywhere on social media and because of this it is easy to get caught up in the façade that the internet creates about love. I am sure at some point throughout the day you see #COUPLESGOALS #MARRIAGEGOALS.

I am a firm believer that your #RELATIONSHIPGOALS should be based on your commitment to each other and what works best for the two of you.

You should strive to create a relationship that is healthy so that your only #GOAL is to impress each other and create a safe haven for your love.

I created the #RELATIONSHIPGOALS journal as an outlet for the two of you to really dig deep into your own love story by being intentional with your thoughts and emotions while putting those feelings on paper.

YOUR RELATIONSHIP! YOUR RULES!

XOXO,
Jen

OUR NAMES:

....

ANNIVERSARY DATE:

....

MONTH 1

IF YOU COULD PRESS A BUTTON AND CHANGE OUR RELATIONSHIP/ MARRIAGE, HOW WOULD IT CHANGE?

MONTH 1 CHALLENGE

This month I challenge you to sit down together and plan out 12 date night ideas that are new for the two of you.
(Don't worry, I have included a list of suggestions.)

Use this challenge to work together to research upcoming events, concerts, cooking classes, etc. in your area. If one of you suggests a date night that is out of your comfort zone don't immediately say no, be open to the idea of trying something new and most importantly something the other person is interested in.

Once you have completed the challenge add the date night on the appropriate calendar month throughout the journal.

The calendars are all blank so that no matter what time of year you purchase this journal you can use it for the full 12 months!

HAPPY PLANNING!

DATE IDEAS:

1. Visit a farmer's market
2. Go to a karaoke bar
3. Have a game night
4. Go camping
5. Recreate your first date ✓
6. Make a personalized scavenger hunt for each other
7. Watch a movie at the drive in ✓
8. Get a couple's massage
9. Do something you have never done before ✓
10. Plan a picnic

1. Visit a local carnival ✓
2. Volunteer together
3. Take a road trip
4. Get matching tattoos
5. Take a yoga class
6. Race go carts
7. Take a workout class together
8. (8.) Take a cooking class together
9. (9.) Visit a gun range
10. Get dressed up and have professional pictures taken

DATE IDEAS:

1. Go horseback riding
2. Go bowling
3. Create a playlist and slow dance at home
4. Visit a flea market
5. (5.) Take a boat ride — Kayaking
6. Get pedicures together
7. Go roller skating
8. Learn a new skill together
9. (9.) Get your palms read
10. Play mini golf

1. Escape Room
2. Watch the sunset together ✓
3. Go to a pro sporting event
4. Make homemade pizza
5. Stay at a bed and breakfast
6. Take a tour of your city
7. Have a movie marathon with popcorn
8. Go on a hot air balloon ride ✓
9. Take an improv class
10. Visit an art gallery

DATE IDEAS:

1. Create a vision board together
2. Go wine tasting
3. (3.) Go bike riding — Segways
4. Get dressed up and go tour million-dollar homes
5. Visit a sex toy shop
6. Go to Costco or Sam's Club on sample day
7. Double date with another couple
8. Take a candle lit bubble bath together
9. Play truth or dare
10. (10.) Take an art class — paint or clay

Year OF DATES

Month: September	Month:	Month:	Month:
Activity:	Activity:	Activity:	Activity:
Dress Up or Casual:	Dress Up or Casual:	Dress Up or Casual:	Dress Up or Casual:
NOTES:	NOTES:	NOTES:	NOTES:

Month:	Month:	Month:	Month:
Activity:	Activity:	Activity:	Activity:
Dress Up or Casual:	Dress Up or Casual:	Dress Up or Casual:	Dress Up or Casual:
NOTES:	NOTES:	NOTES:	NOTES:

Month:	Month:	Month:	Month:
Activity:	Activity:	Activity:	Activity:
Dress Up or Casual:	Dress Up or Casual:	Dress Up or Casual:	Dress Up or Casual:
NOTES:	NOTES:	NOTES:	NOTES:

While interviewing a married woman of 11 years she said something that really stood out to me: "I work a full-time job where I am laser focused on climbing the corporate ladder and I am a full-time student working on my Master's Degree. I am also mom to 3 girls who are involved in tons of activities. Some days, by the time I see my husband I am just tired and want to relax alone. It's not that he has done anything wrong, I simply don't want to be bothered. Before you know it one tired night has turned into two and the next thing you know it's been a week since I actually took the time to kiss him passionately or bury my head in his chest and just love on him. Since it's not anything intentional, when he brings it up, I say, "I honestly just don't remember, I mean, it's not like I'm keeping track! "

Making your relationship intimate and special is the responsibility of both partners. Practice little acts of affection, gratitude, and enjoy physical intimacy as much as possible to strengthen your relationship.

I have included an intimacy tracker that you will use to document your daily affections for each other so you can be sure that no matter how busy you may become you won't let the days pass without showing love to each other.

Intimacy TRACKER

DOCUMENT YOUR DAILY AFFECTIONS FOR EACH OTHER

MONTH..........

SUNDAY	MONDAY	TUESDAY	WEDNESDAY	THURSDAY	FRIDAY	SATURDAY

WEEKLY RELATIONSHIP MEETING

Have you ever been in the middle of a disagreement about one thing and out of nowhere your significant other brings up another issue totally out of left field and you are standing there wondering:

1. Where did this come from?

2. What does this have to do with anything we are talking about right now?

Often times when someone blows up over something "seemingly small" it is part of a much bigger problem. It is so important in a relationship to have intentional conversations about your lives together on a regular basis so that any issues that need to be addressed are addressed in real time and not in the heat of discussion about something else.

I created the Weekly Relationship Meeting as a way for my husband and I to make sure we are addressing any possible underlying issues we may have. It is also a time to give praise to the other person and look back on what worked or needs improvement for the upcoming week.

Choose a day that works best for the two of you to sit together and have your weekly meeting. For us Sunday night after the kids are in bed is the best time, but for you it could be Thursday's because of your work schedules. This is simply about carving time out once a week to sit together and reflect and prepare for what's to come.

Having these weekly meetings has done wonders for our relationship and we know it can do the same for yours!

WEEKLY RELATIONSHIP MEETING

WEEK OF #1 THURSDAY 9-26-19

BOTH OF YOU TAKE TURNS TELLING EACH OTHER SOMETHING POSITIVE ABOUT ONE ANOTHER:

Rebecca has worked really hard to support me as my wife. She helps support the household. She puts in overtime, works sick, injured, and in pain. Rebecca has lossed a noticible amout of weight and I want her to know I'm proud of her. My wife His the most beautiful women on earth. Rebecca listens to me and always has my back.

HOW ARE YOU DOING AS INDIVIDUALS? IS SOMETHING WEIGHING ON YOU OUTSIDE OF YOUR HOME?

My job as usual and money

WHAT ARE YOUR HIGH POINTS OF THE WEEK AS A COUPLE?

On Saturday we had the day off together. I got to spend time with my wife just relaxing and enjoying each others company.
I feel were communicating more. And were both looking forward to the new date night ideas.
I made love to my wife

WHAT ARE YOUR LOW POINTS OF THE WEEK AS A COUPLE?

My ability to listen to Rebecca and take any criticism she may have with a level headed optimistic attitude. My immediate response to Rebecca caused a fight.

WHAT IS THE ONE THING YOU WANT THE OTHER PERSON TO WORK ON THIS COMING WEEK?

I want Rebecca to put her laundrey away the day it's folded on the dresser.

WHAT IMPORTANT EVENTS, MEETINGS, OR OBLIGATIONS DO YOU HAVE THIS WEEK?

Looking forward to our next date night

FOLLOW UP:

DID YOU WORK ON THE ISSUES THAT WERE ADDRESSED LAST WEEK?

WEEKLY RELATIONSHIP MEETING

WEEK OF #2 Friday 10-4-19

BOTH OF YOU TAKE TURNS TELLING EACH OTHER SOMETHING POSITIVE ABOUT ONE ANOTHER:
Rebecca is letting her hair out more. And its beautiful. Smart, sexy. Rebecca has a awesome tan.

HOW ARE YOU DOING AS INDIVIDUALS? IS SOMETHING WEIGHING ON YOU OUTSIDE OF YOUR HOME?
I took Jerry dying this week a little hard. Life is short. You really never know how much time you have. Have to make the best of life regardless of your situation. But be happy. And Rebecca makes me happy

WHAT ARE YOUR HIGH POINTS OF THE WEEK AS A COUPLE?
Poker night has been really fun. I get to spend time interacting with my wife. We have not had 1 serious fight this week.

WHAT ARE YOUR LOW POINTS OF THE WEEK AS A COUPLE?
I need to make eye contact with Rebecca more. I can't or it's hard for me to carry on a conversation when I'm cooking or doing tasks. I need to focus on whats important.

WHAT IS THE ONE THING YOU WANT THE OTHER PERSON TO WORK ON THIS COMING WEEK?
Not leaving dirty dishes in the sink when it's nice and clean. For Rebecca to tell me whats bothering her instead of expecting me to know. Other words > be patient

WHAT IMPORTANT EVENTS, MEETINGS, OR OBLIGATIONS DO YOU HAVE THIS WEEK?
Sunday's state fair. I want Rebecca to wear her yellow dress.

FOLLOW UP:

DID YOU WORK ON THE ISSUES THAT WERE ADDRESSED LAST WEEK?
Yes Rebecca is putting her laundry away. I have been listening more clearly and trying to prevent fights

WEEKLY RELATIONSHIP MEETING

WEEK OF ....

BOTH OF YOU TAKE TURNS TELLING EACH OTHER SOMETHING POSITIVE ABOUT ONE ANOTHER:

HOW ARE YOU DOING AS INDIVIDUALS? IS SOMETHING WEIGHING ON YOU OUTSIDE OF YOUR HOME?

WHAT ARE YOUR HIGH POINTS OF THE WEEK AS A COUPLE?

WHAT ARE YOUR LOW POINTS OF THE WEEK AS A COUPLE?

WHAT IS THE ONE THING YOU WANT THE OTHER PERSON TO WORK ON THIS COMING WEEK?

WHAT IMPORTANT EVENTS, MEETINGS, OR OBLIGATIONS DO YOU HAVE THIS WEEK?

FOLLOW UP:

DID YOU WORK ON THE ISSUES THAT WERE ADDRESSED LAST WEEK?

WEEKLY RELATIONSHIP MEETING

WEEK OF ....

BOTH OF YOU TAKE TURNS TELLING EACH OTHER SOMETHING POSITIVE ABOUT ONE ANOTHER:

HOW ARE YOU DOING AS INDIVIDUALS? IS SOMETHING WEIGHING ON YOU OUTSIDE OF YOUR HOME?

WHAT ARE YOUR HIGH POINTS OF THE WEEK AS A COUPLE?

WHAT ARE YOUR LOW POINTS OF THE WEEK AS A COUPLE?

WHAT IS THE ONE THING YOU WANT THE OTHER PERSON TO WORK ON THIS COMING WEEK?

WHAT IMPORTANT EVENTS, MEETINGS, OR OBLIGATIONS DO YOU HAVE THIS WEEK?

FOLLOW UP:

DID YOU WORK ON THE ISSUES THAT WERE ADDRESSED LAST WEEK?

Let's talk about it!

MONTH 2

WHAT'S YOUR HAPPIEST MEMORY OF US TOGETHER?

COUPLE'S INTERVIEW

Getting advice from other married or deeply committed couples that you both respect can provide vital perspective on what it is like to be married or committed for a long time.

During the course of this journal you will interview 6 married or deeply committed couples to see what their lives are like away from the highlight reel that social media shows. Choose couples who you feel will open up to you and who want to see your relationship flourish. Once the interview is over (don't worry I have provided the questions) you will write down 5 things you learned that could make your own relationship or marriage better. I also want you to write down anything that you feel were red flags that perhaps the two of you need to address in your own relationship.

COUPLE'S INTERVIEW:

HOW DID YOU MEET?

HOW LONG DID YOU DATE BEFORE YOU KNEW THIS WAS THE PERSON YOU WANT TO SPEND THE REST OF YOUR LIFE WITH?

WHAT WAS IT ABOUT THE OTHER PERSON THAT MADE THEM DIFFERENT FROM ANYONE ELSE YOU HAD EVER BEEN WITH?

HOW DO YOU "FIGHT" FAIR?

DO YOU BELIEVE IN GENDER ROLES WHEN IT COMES TO CHORES IN YOUR HOUSEHOLD?

WHAT DO YOU THINK THE MOST CHALLENGING PART ABOUT BEING MARRIED/IN A COMMITTED RELATIONSHIP IS?

COUPLE'S INTERVIEW:

WHAT IS THE BEST ADVICE YOU RECEIVED THAT HELPED YOU THROUGH ROUGH TIMES OR HELPED YOU PREVENT ROUGH TIMES?

DO YOU "LIKE" EACH OTHER EVERY DAY?

DO YOU EVER FEEL BORED WITH YOUR RELATIONSHIP? IF SO, WHAT STEPS DO YOU TAKE TO SPICE THINGS UP?

DO YOU GET ALONG WITH YOUR IN-LAWS? IF NOT, HOW DOES THAT EFFECT YOUR MARRIAGE/RELATIONSHIP?

WHO HANDLES THE FINANCES AND WHY?

COMPLETE THIS SENTENCE: THE BEST PART OF OUR LIFE TOGETHER IS.......

Intimacy TRACKER

DOCUMENT YOUR DAILY AFFECTIONS FOR EACH OTHER

MONTH ....

SUNDAY	MONDAY	TUESDAY	WEDNESDAY	THURSDAY	FRIDAY	SATURDAY

WEEKLY RELATIONSHIP MEETING

WEEK OF ....

BOTH OF YOU TAKE TURNS TELLING EACH OTHER SOMETHING POSITIVE ABOUT ONE ANOTHER:

HOW ARE YOU DOING AS INDIVIDUALS? IS SOMETHING WEIGHING ON YOU OUTSIDE OF YOUR HOME?

WHAT ARE YOUR HIGH POINTS OF THE WEEK AS A COUPLE?

WHAT ARE YOUR LOW POINTS OF THE WEEK AS A COUPLE?

WHAT IS THE ONE THING YOU WANT THE OTHER PERSON TO WORK ON THIS COMING WEEK?

WHAT IMPORTANT EVENTS, MEETINGS, OR OBLIGATIONS DO YOU HAVE THIS WEEK?

FOLLOW UP:

DID YOU WORK ON THE ISSUES THAT WERE ADDRESSED LAST WEEK?

WEEKLY RELATIONSHIP MEETING

WEEK OF ....

BOTH OF YOU TAKE TURNS TELLING EACH OTHER SOMETHING POSITIVE ABOUT ONE ANOTHER:

HOW ARE YOU DOING AS INDIVIDUALS? IS SOMETHING WEIGHING ON YOU OUTSIDE OF YOUR HOME?

WHAT ARE YOUR HIGH POINTS OF THE WEEK AS A COUPLE?

WHAT ARE YOUR LOW POINTS OF THE WEEK AS A COUPLE?

WHAT IS THE ONE THING YOU WANT THE OTHER PERSON TO WORK ON THIS COMING WEEK?

WHAT IMPORTANT EVENTS, MEETINGS, OR OBLIGATIONS DO YOU HAVE THIS WEEK?

FOLLOW UP:

DID YOU WORK ON THE ISSUES THAT WERE ADDRESSED LAST WEEK?

WEEKLY RELATIONSHIP MEETING

WEEK OF ....

BOTH OF YOU TAKE TURNS TELLING EACH OTHER SOMETHING POSITIVE ABOUT ONE ANOTHER:

HOW ARE YOU DOING AS INDIVIDUALS? IS SOMETHING WEIGHING ON YOU OUTSIDE OF YOUR HOME?

WHAT ARE YOUR HIGH POINTS OF THE WEEK AS A COUPLE?

WHAT ARE YOUR LOW POINTS OF THE WEEK AS A COUPLE?

WHAT IS THE ONE THING YOU WANT THE OTHER PERSON TO WORK ON THIS COMING WEEK?

WHAT IMPORTANT EVENTS, MEETINGS, OR OBLIGATIONS DO YOU HAVE THIS WEEK?

FOLLOW UP:

DID YOU WORK ON THE ISSUES THAT WERE ADDRESSED LAST WEEK?

WEEKLY RELATIONSHIP MEETING

WEEK OF ....

BOTH OF YOU TAKE TURNS TELLING EACH OTHER SOMETHING POSITIVE ABOUT ONE ANOTHER:

HOW ARE YOU DOING AS INDIVIDUALS? IS SOMETHING WEIGHING ON YOU OUTSIDE OF YOUR HOME?

WHAT ARE YOUR HIGH POINTS OF THE WEEK AS A COUPLE?

WHAT ARE YOUR LOW POINTS OF THE WEEK AS A COUPLE?

WHAT IS THE ONE THING YOU WANT THE OTHER PERSON TO WORK ON THIS COMING WEEK?

WHAT IMPORTANT EVENTS, MEETINGS, OR OBLIGATIONS DO YOU HAVE THIS WEEK?

FOLLOW UP:

DID YOU WORK ON THE ISSUES THAT WERE ADDRESSED LAST WEEK?

Let's talk about it!

....

....

....

....

....

....

....

....

....

....

....

....

....

....

....

....

....

....

....

MONTH 3

WHAT WOULD YOU CONSIDER UNFORGIVEABLE AND WHY?

MONTH 3 CHALLENGE

Finances, budgeting and spending habits are all words that would make me cringe before my husband and I took control of our money.

Living paycheck to paycheck and struggling to pay bills can cause some serious arguments if you aren't careful. The challenge for this month is to sit down together and create a budget and savings plan for your future. I have included a template for you to follow complete with a simple plan to save $1,000 for your rainy-day fund.

Budget Tracker

EXPENSES	BUDGET	ACTUAL
SUBTOTALS:		

INCOME 1

+

INCOME 2

+

OTHER INCOME

=

TOTAL INCOME

−

TOTAL ACTUAL EXPENSES

=

REMAINING BALANCE

12 WEEKS TO $1,000 RAINY DAY FUND

WEEK	DATE	DEPOSIT	BALANCE	
1		$60	$60	☐
2		$80	$140	☐
3		$90	$230	☐
4		$100	$330	☐
5		$65	$395	☐
6		$80	$475	☐
7		$90	$565	☐
8		$100	$665	☐
9		$65	$730	☐
10		$80	$810	☐
11		$90	$900	☐
12		$100	$1000	☐

Intimacy TRACKER

DOCUMENT YOUR DAILY AFFECTIONS FOR EACH OTHER

MONTH ....

SUNDAY	MONDAY	TUESDAY	WEDNESDAY	THURSDAY	FRIDAY	SATURDAY

WEEKLY RELATIONSHIP MEETING

WEEK OF ....

BOTH OF YOU TAKE TURNS TELLING EACH OTHER SOMETHING POSITIVE ABOUT ONE ANOTHER:

HOW ARE YOU DOING AS INDIVIDUALS? IS SOMETHING WEIGHING ON YOU OUTSIDE OF YOUR HOME?

WHAT ARE YOUR HIGH POINTS OF THE WEEK AS A COUPLE?

WHAT ARE YOUR LOW POINTS OF THE WEEK AS A COUPLE?

WHAT IS THE ONE THING YOU WANT THE OTHER PERSON TO WORK ON THIS COMING WEEK?

WHAT IMPORTANT EVENTS, MEETINGS, OR OBLIGATIONS DO YOU HAVE THIS WEEK?

FOLLOW UP:

DID YOU WORK ON THE ISSUES THAT WERE ADDRESSED LAST WEEK?

WEEKLY RELATIONSHIP MEETING

WEEK OF ....

BOTH OF YOU TAKE TURNS TELLING EACH OTHER SOMETHING POSITIVE ABOUT ONE ANOTHER:

HOW ARE YOU DOING AS INDIVIDUALS? IS SOMETHING WEIGHING ON YOU OUTSIDE OF YOUR HOME?

WHAT ARE YOUR HIGH POINTS OF THE WEEK AS A COUPLE?

WHAT ARE YOUR LOW POINTS OF THE WEEK AS A COUPLE?

WHAT IS THE ONE THING YOU WANT THE OTHER PERSON TO WORK ON THIS COMING WEEK?

WHAT IMPORTANT EVENTS, MEETINGS, OR OBLIGATIONS DO YOU HAVE THIS WEEK?

FOLLOW UP:

DID YOU WORK ON THE ISSUES THAT WERE ADDRESSED LAST WEEK?

WEEKLY RELATIONSHIP MEETING

WEEK OF ....

BOTH OF YOU TAKE TURNS TELLING EACH OTHER SOMETHING POSITIVE ABOUT ONE ANOTHER:

HOW ARE YOU DOING AS INDIVIDUALS? IS SOMETHING WEIGHING ON YOU OUTSIDE OF YOUR HOME?

WHAT ARE YOUR HIGH POINTS OF THE WEEK AS A COUPLE?

WHAT ARE YOUR LOW POINTS OF THE WEEK AS A COUPLE?

WHAT IS THE ONE THING YOU WANT THE OTHER PERSON TO WORK ON THIS COMING WEEK?

WHAT IMPORTANT EVENTS, MEETINGS, OR OBLIGATIONS DO YOU HAVE THIS WEEK?

FOLLOW UP:

DID YOU WORK ON THE ISSUES THAT WERE ADDRESSED LAST WEEK?

WEEKLY RELATIONSHIP MEETING

WEEK OF ....

BOTH OF YOU TAKE TURNS TELLING EACH OTHER SOMETHING POSITIVE ABOUT ONE ANOTHER:

HOW ARE YOU DOING AS INDIVIDUALS? IS SOMETHING WEIGHING ON YOU OUTSIDE OF YOUR HOME?

WHAT ARE YOUR HIGH POINTS OF THE WEEK AS A COUPLE?

WHAT ARE YOUR LOW POINTS OF THE WEEK AS A COUPLE?

WHAT IS THE ONE THING YOU WANT THE OTHER PERSON TO WORK ON THIS COMING WEEK?

WHAT IMPORTANT EVENTS, MEETINGS, OR OBLIGATIONS DO YOU HAVE THIS WEEK?

FOLLOW UP:

DID YOU WORK ON THE ISSUES THAT WERE ADDRESSED LAST WEEK?

Let's talk about it!

MONTH 4

CAN YOU THINK OF AN EXAMPLE OF A CONFLICT WE HAD THAT YOU FELT WE DEALT WITH SUCCESSFULLY?

COUPLE'S INTERVIEW:

HOW DID YOU MEET?

HOW LONG DID YOU DATE BEFORE YOU KNEW THIS WAS THE PERSON YOU WANT TO SPEND THE REST OF YOUR LIFE WITH?

WHAT WAS IT ABOUT THE OTHER PERSON THAT MADE THEM DIFFERENT FROM ANYONE ELSE YOU HAD EVER BEEN WITH?

HOW DO YOU "FIGHT" FAIR?

DO YOU BELIEVE IN GENDER ROLES WHEN IT COMES TO CHORES IN YOUR HOUSEHOLD?

WHAT DO YOU THINK THE MOST CHALLENGING PART ABOUT BEING MARRIED/IN A COMMITTED RELATIONSHIP IS?

COUPLE'S INTERVIEW:

WHAT IS THE BEST ADVICE YOU RECEIVED THAT HELPED YOU THROUGH ROUGH TIMES OR HELPED YOU PREVENT ROUGH TIMES?

DO YOU "LIKE" EACH OTHER EVERY DAY?

DO YOU EVER FEEL BORED WITH YOUR RELATIONSHIP? IF SO, WHAT STEPS DO YOU TAKE TO SPICE THINGS UP?

DO YOU GET ALONG WITH YOUR IN-LAWS? IF NOT, HOW DOES THAT EFFECT YOUR MARRIAGE/RELATIONSHIP?

WHO HANDLES THE FINANCES AND WHY?

COMPLETE THIS SENTENCE: THE BEST PART OF OUR LIFE TOGETHER IS.......

Intimacy TRACKER
DOCUMENT YOUR DAILY AFFECTIONS FOR EACH OTHER

MONTH..............

SUNDAY	MONDAY	TUESDAY	WEDNESDAY	THURSDAY	FRIDAY	SATURDAY

WEEKLY RELATIONSHIP MEETING

WEEK OF ....

BOTH OF YOU TAKE TURNS TELLING EACH OTHER SOMETHING POSITIVE ABOUT ONE ANOTHER:

HOW ARE YOU DOING AS INDIVIDUALS? IS SOMETHING WEIGHING ON YOU OUTSIDE OF YOUR HOME?

WHAT ARE YOUR HIGH POINTS OF THE WEEK AS A COUPLE?

WHAT ARE YOUR LOW POINTS OF THE WEEK AS A COUPLE?

WHAT IS THE ONE THING YOU WANT THE OTHER PERSON TO WORK ON THIS COMING WEEK?

WHAT IMPORTANT EVENTS, MEETINGS, OR OBLIGATIONS DO YOU HAVE THIS WEEK?

FOLLOW UP:

DID YOU WORK ON THE ISSUES THAT WERE ADDRESSED LAST WEEK?

WEEKLY RELATIONSHIP MEETING

WEEK OF ....

BOTH OF YOU TAKE TURNS TELLING EACH OTHER SOMETHING POSITIVE ABOUT ONE ANOTHER:

HOW ARE YOU DOING AS INDIVIDUALS? IS SOMETHING WEIGHING ON YOU OUTSIDE OF YOUR HOME?

WHAT ARE YOUR HIGH POINTS OF THE WEEK AS A COUPLE?

WHAT ARE YOUR LOW POINTS OF THE WEEK AS A COUPLE?

WHAT IS THE ONE THING YOU WANT THE OTHER PERSON TO WORK ON THIS COMING WEEK?

WHAT IMPORTANT EVENTS, MEETINGS, OR OBLIGATIONS DO YOU HAVE THIS WEEK?

FOLLOW UP:

DID YOU WORK ON THE ISSUES THAT WERE ADDRESSED LAST WEEK?

WEEKLY RELATIONSHIP MEETING

WEEK OF ....

BOTH OF YOU TAKE TURNS TELLING EACH OTHER SOMETHING POSITIVE ABOUT ONE ANOTHER:

HOW ARE YOU DOING AS INDIVIDUALS? IS SOMETHING WEIGHING ON YOU OUTSIDE OF YOUR HOME?

WHAT ARE YOUR HIGH POINTS OF THE WEEK AS A COUPLE?

WHAT ARE YOUR LOW POINTS OF THE WEEK AS A COUPLE?

WHAT IS THE ONE THING YOU WANT THE OTHER PERSON TO WORK ON THIS COMING WEEK?

WHAT IMPORTANT EVENTS, MEETINGS, OR OBLIGATIONS DO YOU HAVE THIS WEEK?

FOLLOW UP:

DID YOU WORK ON THE ISSUES THAT WERE ADDRESSED LAST WEEK?

WEEKLY RELATIONSHIP MEETING

WEEK OF ....

BOTH OF YOU TAKE TURNS TELLING EACH OTHER SOMETHING POSITIVE ABOUT ONE ANOTHER:

HOW ARE YOU DOING AS INDIVIDUALS? IS SOMETHING WEIGHING ON YOU OUTSIDE OF YOUR HOME?

WHAT ARE YOUR HIGH POINTS OF THE WEEK AS A COUPLE?

WHAT ARE YOUR LOW POINTS OF THE WEEK AS A COUPLE?

WHAT IS THE ONE THING YOU WANT THE OTHER PERSON TO WORK ON THIS COMING WEEK?

WHAT IMPORTANT EVENTS, MEETINGS, OR OBLIGATIONS DO YOU HAVE THIS WEEK?

FOLLOW UP:

DID YOU WORK ON THE ISSUES THAT WERE ADDRESSED LAST WEEK?

Let's talk about it!

MONTH 5

WHAT MAKES YOU FEEL APPRECIATED?

MONTH 5 CHALLENGE

BUCKET LIST

One of the things that I love about being married to my husband is planning for the future. Having something to look forward to like a trip or activity really helps on those days when life or work is getting the best of us.

Your challenge for this month is to come up with a Bucket List of activities or trips. Need some help getting your creative juices flowing? I have included some ideas!

- [ ] Travel the world.
- [ ] Run a marathon.
- [ ] Learn to sutf.
- [ ] Break a world record.
- [ ] Go on a hot air ballon ride.
- [ ] Ride a horse on a beach.
- [ ] Go on a safari.
- [ ] Attend the Olympics.
- [ ] Visit the Grand Canyon.
- [ ] Go scuba diving.
- [ ] Ride in a helicopter.
- [ ] Take a road trip with no planned destination.
- [ ] See the Great Pyramids.
- [ ] Kiss in front of the Eiffel Tower.
- [ ] Visit the ocean and throw in a message in a bottle
- [ ] Walk the Great Wall of China.
- [ ] Hunt for diamonds at Crater of Diamonds State
- [ ] Ride a train across the country.

OUR BUCKET LIST:

....

....

....

....

....

....

....

....

....

....

....

....

....

....

Intimacy TRACKER
DOCUMENT YOUR DAILY AFFECTIONS FOR EACH OTHER

MONTH ....

SUNDAY	MONDAY	TUESDAY	WEDNESDAY	THURSDAY	FRIDAY	SATURDAY

WEEKLY RELATIONSHIP MEETING

WEEK OF ....

BOTH OF YOU TAKE TURNS TELLING EACH OTHER SOMETHING POSITIVE ABOUT ONE ANOTHER:

HOW ARE YOU DOING AS INDIVIDUALS? IS SOMETHING WEIGHING ON YOU OUTSIDE OF YOUR HOME?

WHAT ARE YOUR HIGH POINTS OF THE WEEK AS A COUPLE?

WHAT ARE YOUR LOW POINTS OF THE WEEK AS A COUPLE?

WHAT IS THE ONE THING YOU WANT THE OTHER PERSON TO WORK ON THIS COMING WEEK?

WHAT IMPORTANT EVENTS, MEETINGS, OR OBLIGATIONS DO YOU HAVE THIS WEEK?

FOLLOW UP:

DID YOU WORK ON THE ISSUES THAT WERE ADDRESSED LAST WEEK?

WEEKLY RELATIONSHIP MEETING

WEEK OF ....

BOTH OF YOU TAKE TURNS TELLING EACH OTHER SOMETHING POSITIVE ABOUT ONE ANOTHER:

HOW ARE YOU DOING AS INDIVIDUALS? IS SOMETHING WEIGHING ON YOU OUTSIDE OF YOUR HOME?

WHAT ARE YOUR HIGH POINTS OF THE WEEK AS A COUPLE?

WHAT ARE YOUR LOW POINTS OF THE WEEK AS A COUPLE?

WHAT IS THE ONE THING YOU WANT THE OTHER PERSON TO WORK ON THIS COMING WEEK?

WHAT IMPORTANT EVENTS, MEETINGS, OR OBLIGATIONS DO YOU HAVE THIS WEEK?

FOLLOW UP:

DID YOU WORK ON THE ISSUES THAT WERE ADDRESSED LAST WEEK?

WEEKLY RELATIONSHIP MEETING

WEEK OF ....

BOTH OF YOU TAKE TURNS TELLING EACH OTHER SOMETHING POSITIVE ABOUT ONE ANOTHER:

HOW ARE YOU DOING AS INDIVIDUALS? IS SOMETHING WEIGHING ON YOU OUTSIDE OF YOUR HOME?

WHAT ARE YOUR HIGH POINTS OF THE WEEK AS A COUPLE?

WHAT ARE YOUR LOW POINTS OF THE WEEK AS A COUPLE?

WHAT IS THE ONE THING YOU WANT THE OTHER PERSON TO WORK ON THIS COMING WEEK?

WHAT IMPORTANT EVENTS, MEETINGS, OR OBLIGATIONS DO YOU HAVE THIS WEEK?

FOLLOW UP:

DID YOU WORK ON THE ISSUES THAT WERE ADDRESSED LAST WEEK?

WEEKLY RELATIONSHIP MEETING

WEEK OF ....

BOTH OF YOU TAKE TURNS TELLING EACH OTHER SOMETHING POSITIVE ABOUT ONE ANOTHER:

HOW ARE YOU DOING AS INDIVIDUALS? IS SOMETHING WEIGHING ON YOU OUTSIDE OF YOUR HOME?

WHAT ARE YOUR HIGH POINTS OF THE WEEK AS A COUPLE?

WHAT ARE YOUR LOW POINTS OF THE WEEK AS A COUPLE?

WHAT IS THE ONE THING YOU WANT THE OTHER PERSON TO WORK ON THIS COMING WEEK?

WHAT IMPORTANT EVENTS, MEETINGS, OR OBLIGATIONS DO YOU HAVE THIS WEEK?

FOLLOW UP:

DID YOU WORK ON THE ISSUES THAT WERE ADDRESSED LAST WEEK?

Let's talk about it!

MONTH 6

WHAT IS THE BEST WAY FOR ME TO COMMUNICATE DIFFICULT FEELINGS ABOUT YOU SO THAT YOU ARE NOT OFFENDED?

COUPLE'S INTERVIEW:

HOW DID YOU MEET?

HOW LONG DID YOU DATE BEFORE YOU KNEW THIS WAS THE PERSON YOU WANT TO SPEND THE REST OF YOUR LIFE WITH?

WHAT WAS IT ABOUT THE OTHER PERSON THAT MADE THEM DIFFERENT FROM ANYONE ELSE YOU HAD EVER BEEN WITH?

HOW DO YOU "FIGHT" FAIR?

DO YOU BELIEVE IN GENDER ROLES WHEN IT COMES TO CHORES IN YOUR HOUSEHOLD?

WHAT DO YOU THINK THE MOST CHALLENGING PART ABOUT BEING MARRIED/IN A COMMITTED RELATIONSHIP IS?

COUPLE'S INTERVIEW:

WHAT IS THE BEST ADVICE YOU RECEIVED THAT HELPED YOU THROUGH ROUGH TIMES OR HELPED YOU PREVENT ROUGH TIMES?

DO YOU "LIKE" EACH OTHER EVERY DAY?

DO YOU EVER FEEL BORED WITH YOUR RELATIONSHIP? IF SO, WHAT STEPS DO YOU TAKE TO SPICE THINGS UP?

DO YOU GET ALONG WITH YOUR IN-LAWS? IF NOT, HOW DOES THAT EFFECT YOUR MARRIAGE/RELATIONSHIP?

WHO HANDLES THE FINANCES AND WHY?

COMPLETE THIS SENTENCE: THE BEST PART OF OUR LIFE TOGETHER IS.......

Intimacy TRACKER

DOCUMENT YOUR DAILY AFFECTIONS FOR EACH OTHER

MONTH ....

SUNDAY	MONDAY	TUESDAY	WEDNESDAY	THURSDAY	FRIDAY	SATURDAY

WEEKLY RELATIONSHIP MEETING

WEEK OF ....

BOTH OF YOU TAKE TURNS TELLING EACH OTHER SOMETHING POSITIVE ABOUT ONE ANOTHER:

HOW ARE YOU DOING AS INDIVIDUALS? IS SOMETHING WEIGHING ON YOU OUTSIDE OF YOUR HOME?

WHAT ARE YOUR HIGH POINTS OF THE WEEK AS A COUPLE?

WHAT ARE YOUR LOW POINTS OF THE WEEK AS A COUPLE?

WHAT IS THE ONE THING YOU WANT THE OTHER PERSON TO WORK ON THIS COMING WEEK?

WHAT IMPORTANT EVENTS, MEETINGS, OR OBLIGATIONS DO YOU HAVE THIS WEEK?

FOLLOW UP:

DID YOU WORK ON THE ISSUES THAT WERE ADDRESSED LAST WEEK?

WEEKLY RELATIONSHIP MEETING

WEEK OF ....

BOTH OF YOU TAKE TURNS TELLING EACH OTHER SOMETHING POSITIVE ABOUT ONE ANOTHER:

HOW ARE YOU DOING AS INDIVIDUALS? IS SOMETHING WEIGHING ON YOU OUTSIDE OF YOUR HOME?

WHAT ARE YOUR HIGH POINTS OF THE WEEK AS A COUPLE?

WHAT ARE YOUR LOW POINTS OF THE WEEK AS A COUPLE?

WHAT IS THE ONE THING YOU WANT THE OTHER PERSON TO WORK ON THIS COMING WEEK?

WHAT IMPORTANT EVENTS, MEETINGS, OR OBLIGATIONS DO YOU HAVE THIS WEEK?

FOLLOW UP:

DID YOU WORK ON THE ISSUES THAT WERE ADDRESSED LAST WEEK?

WEEKLY RELATIONSHIP MEETING

WEEK OF ....

BOTH OF YOU TAKE TURNS TELLING EACH OTHER SOMETHING POSITIVE ABOUT ONE ANOTHER:

HOW ARE YOU DOING AS INDIVIDUALS? IS SOMETHING WEIGHING ON YOU OUTSIDE OF YOUR HOME?

WHAT ARE YOUR HIGH POINTS OF THE WEEK AS A COUPLE?

WHAT ARE YOUR LOW POINTS OF THE WEEK AS A COUPLE?

WHAT IS THE ONE THING YOU WANT THE OTHER PERSON TO WORK ON THIS COMING WEEK?

WHAT IMPORTANT EVENTS, MEETINGS, OR OBLIGATIONS DO YOU HAVE THIS WEEK?

FOLLOW UP:

DID YOU WORK ON THE ISSUES THAT WERE ADDRESSED LAST WEEK?

WEEKLY RELATIONSHIP MEETING

WEEK OF ....

BOTH OF YOU TAKE TURNS TELLING EACH OTHER SOMETHING POSITIVE ABOUT ONE ANOTHER:

HOW ARE YOU DOING AS INDIVIDUALS? IS SOMETHING WEIGHING ON YOU OUTSIDE OF YOUR HOME?

WHAT ARE YOUR HIGH POINTS OF THE WEEK AS A COUPLE?

WHAT ARE YOUR LOW POINTS OF THE WEEK AS A COUPLE?

WHAT IS THE ONE THING YOU WANT THE OTHER PERSON TO WORK ON THIS COMING WEEK?

WHAT IMPORTANT EVENTS, MEETINGS, OR OBLIGATIONS DO YOU HAVE THIS WEEK?

FOLLOW UP:

DID YOU WORK ON THE ISSUES THAT WERE ADDRESSED LAST WEEK?

Let's talk about it!

....

....

....

....

....

....

....

....

....

....

....

....

....

....

....

....

....

MONTH 7

WHAT HAS BEEN YOUR GREATEST ACCOMPLISHMENT THIS YEAR?

MONTH 7 CHALLENGE

Being in a marriage/relationship means that sometimes you have to do things you may not want to do. My husband knows I despise the grocery store so he does all of the shopping. I also know that he cannot handle vomit AT ALL so when one of the kiddos pukes, guess whose job it is to clean it up? That's right mine. I don't do it because I love throw up, I do it because I know that it isn't something that he wants to do.

The challenge for this month is to do 5 chores/tasks for the other person. If one of you always cooks dinner or folds the clothes then switch. Putting yourself in the other persons shoes can really give you a new level of appreciation for all that they do on a daily basis.

I have included a chore swapping chart and an easy daily cleaning chart to help your day to day run smoother

Easiest cleaning schedule

daily

- MAKE BEDS
- 1 LOAD OF LAUDRY: START TO FINISH
- DISHWASHER
- WIPE DOWN KITCHEN COUNTERS, SINK, STOVETOP, & TABLE
- QUICK PICK-UP

weekly

monday
- DUST, SWEEP, VACUUM, MOP

tuesday
- CLEAN BATHROOMS

wednesday
- WIPE OFF CABINENTS & WALLS

thursday
- SWEEP, VACUUM, MOP

friday
- DECLUTTER + CLEAN BEDROOMS
- WASH BEDDING

Daily CHORE SWAP

WRITE DOWN YOUR 3 MAIN CHORES AND SWAP

MY CHORES

....

....

....

YOUR CHORES

....

....

....

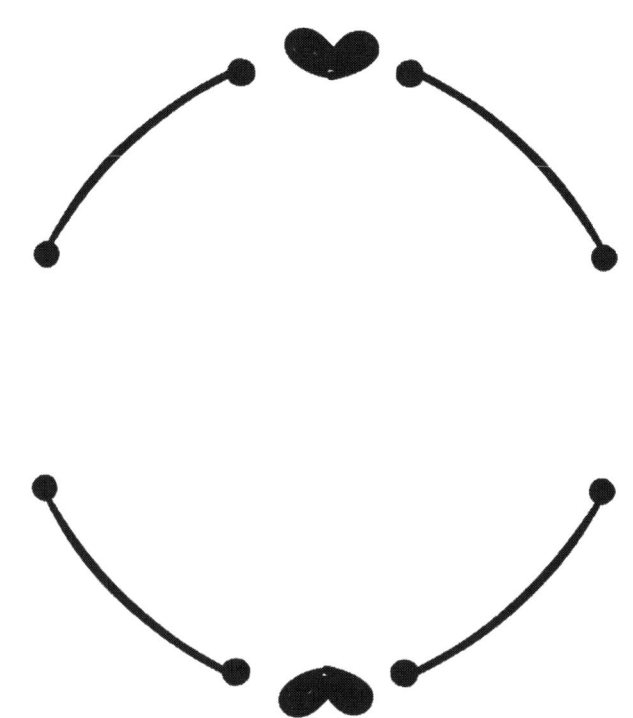

Intimacy TRACKER
DOCUMENT YOUR DAILY AFFECTIONS FOR EACH OTHER

MONTH ....

SUNDAY	MONDAY	TUESDAY	WEDNESDAY	THURSDAY	FRIDAY	SATURDAY

WEEKLY RELATIONSHIP MEETING

WEEK OF ....

BOTH OF YOU TAKE TURNS TELLING EACH OTHER SOMETHING POSITIVE ABOUT ONE ANOTHER:

HOW ARE YOU DOING AS INDIVIDUALS? IS SOMETHING WEIGHING ON YOU OUTSIDE OF YOUR HOME?

WHAT ARE YOUR HIGH POINTS OF THE WEEK AS A COUPLE?

WHAT ARE YOUR LOW POINTS OF THE WEEK AS A COUPLE?

WHAT IS THE ONE THING YOU WANT THE OTHER PERSON TO WORK ON THIS COMING WEEK?

WHAT IMPORTANT EVENTS, MEETINGS, OR OBLIGATIONS DO YOU HAVE THIS WEEK?

FOLLOW UP:

DID YOU WORK ON THE ISSUES THAT WERE ADDRESSED LAST WEEK?

WEEKLY RELATIONSHIP MEETING

WEEK OF ....

BOTH OF YOU TAKE TURNS TELLING EACH OTHER SOMETHING POSITIVE ABOUT ONE ANOTHER:

HOW ARE YOU DOING AS INDIVIDUALS? IS SOMETHING WEIGHING ON YOU OUTSIDE OF YOUR HOME?

WHAT ARE YOUR HIGH POINTS OF THE WEEK AS A COUPLE?

WHAT ARE YOUR LOW POINTS OF THE WEEK AS A COUPLE?

WHAT IS THE ONE THING YOU WANT THE OTHER PERSON TO WORK ON THIS COMING WEEK?

WHAT IMPORTANT EVENTS, MEETINGS, OR OBLIGATIONS DO YOU HAVE THIS WEEK?

FOLLOW UP:

DID YOU WORK ON THE ISSUES THAT WERE ADDRESSED LAST WEEK?

WEEKLY RELATIONSHIP MEETING

WEEK OF ....

BOTH OF YOU TAKE TURNS TELLING EACH OTHER SOMETHING POSITIVE ABOUT ONE ANOTHER:

HOW ARE YOU DOING AS INDIVIDUALS? IS SOMETHING WEIGHING ON YOU OUTSIDE OF YOUR HOME?

WHAT ARE YOUR HIGH POINTS OF THE WEEK AS A COUPLE?

WHAT ARE YOUR LOW POINTS OF THE WEEK AS A COUPLE?

WHAT IS THE ONE THING YOU WANT THE OTHER PERSON TO WORK ON THIS COMING WEEK?

WHAT IMPORTANT EVENTS, MEETINGS, OR OBLIGATIONS DO YOU HAVE THIS WEEK?

FOLLOW UP:

DID YOU WORK ON THE ISSUES THAT WERE ADDRESSED LAST WEEK?

WEEKLY RELATIONSHIP MEETING

WEEK OF ....

BOTH OF YOU TAKE TURNS TELLING EACH OTHER SOMETHING POSITIVE ABOUT ONE ANOTHER:

HOW ARE YOU DOING AS INDIVIDUALS? IS SOMETHING WEIGHING ON YOU OUTSIDE OF YOUR HOME?

WHAT ARE YOUR HIGH POINTS OF THE WEEK AS A COUPLE?

WHAT ARE YOUR LOW POINTS OF THE WEEK AS A COUPLE?

WHAT IS THE ONE THING YOU WANT THE OTHER PERSON TO WORK ON THIS COMING WEEK?

WHAT IMPORTANT EVENTS, MEETINGS, OR OBLIGATIONS DO YOU HAVE THIS WEEK?

FOLLOW UP:

DID YOU WORK ON THE ISSUES THAT WERE ADDRESSED LAST WEEK?

Let's talk about it!

MONTH 8

WHAT IS YOUR FAVORITE DATE WE'VE HAD? WHY?

COUPLE'S INTERVIEW:

HOW DID YOU MEET?

HOW LONG DID YOU DATE BEFORE YOU KNEW THIS WAS THE PERSON YOU WANT TO SPEND THE REST OF YOUR LIFE WITH?

WHAT WAS IT ABOUT THE OTHER PERSON THAT MADE THEM DIFFERENT FROM ANYONE ELSE YOU HAD EVER BEEN WITH?

HOW DO YOU "FIGHT" FAIR?

DO YOU BELIEVE IN GENDER ROLES WHEN IT COMES TO CHORES IN YOUR HOUSEHOLD?

WHAT DO YOU THINK THE MOST CHALLENGING PART ABOUT BEING MARRIED/IN A COMMITTED RELATIONSHIP IS?

COUPLE'S INTERVIEW:

WHAT IS THE BEST ADVICE YOU RECEIVED THAT HELPED YOU THROUGH ROUGH TIMES OR HELPED YOU PREVENT ROUGH TIMES?

DO YOU "LIKE" EACH OTHER EVERY DAY?

DO YOU EVER FEEL BORED WITH YOUR RELATIONSHIP? IF SO, WHAT STEPS DO YOU TAKE TO SPICE THINGS UP?

DO YOU GET ALONG WITH YOUR IN-LAWS? IF NOT, HOW DOES THAT EFFECT YOUR MARRIAGE/RELATIONSHIP?

WHO HANDLES THE FINANCES AND WHY?

COMPLETE THIS SENTENCE: THE BEST PART OF OUR LIFE TOGETHER IS.......

Intimacy TRACKER

DOCUMENT YOUR DAILY AFFECTIONS FOR EACH OTHER

MONTH..........

SUNDAY	MONDAY	TUESDAY	WEDNESDAY	THURSDAY	FRIDAY	SATURDAY

WEEKLY RELATIONSHIP MEETING

WEEK OF ....

BOTH OF YOU TAKE TURNS TELLING EACH OTHER SOMETHING POSITIVE ABOUT ONE ANOTHER:

HOW ARE YOU DOING AS INDIVIDUALS? IS SOMETHING WEIGHING ON YOU OUTSIDE OF YOUR HOME?

WHAT ARE YOUR HIGH POINTS OF THE WEEK AS A COUPLE?

WHAT ARE YOUR LOW POINTS OF THE WEEK AS A COUPLE?

WHAT IS THE ONE THING YOU WANT THE OTHER PERSON TO WORK ON THIS COMING WEEK?

WHAT IMPORTANT EVENTS, MEETINGS, OR OBLIGATIONS DO YOU HAVE THIS WEEK?

FOLLOW UP:

DID YOU WORK ON THE ISSUES THAT WERE ADDRESSED LAST WEEK?

WEEKLY RELATIONSHIP MEETING

WEEK OF ....

BOTH OF YOU TAKE TURNS TELLING EACH OTHER SOMETHING POSITIVE ABOUT ONE ANOTHER:

HOW ARE YOU DOING AS INDIVIDUALS? IS SOMETHING WEIGHING ON YOU OUTSIDE OF YOUR HOME?

WHAT ARE YOUR HIGH POINTS OF THE WEEK AS A COUPLE?

WHAT ARE YOUR LOW POINTS OF THE WEEK AS A COUPLE?

WHAT IS THE ONE THING YOU WANT THE OTHER PERSON TO WORK ON THIS COMING WEEK?

WHAT IMPORTANT EVENTS, MEETINGS, OR OBLIGATIONS DO YOU HAVE THIS WEEK?

FOLLOW UP:

DID YOU WORK ON THE ISSUES THAT WERE ADDRESSED LAST WEEK?

WEEKLY RELATIONSHIP MEETING

WEEK OF ....

BOTH OF YOU TAKE TURNS TELLING EACH OTHER SOMETHING POSITIVE ABOUT ONE ANOTHER:

HOW ARE YOU DOING AS INDIVIDUALS? IS SOMETHING WEIGHING ON YOU OUTSIDE OF YOUR HOME?

WHAT ARE YOUR HIGH POINTS OF THE WEEK AS A COUPLE?

WHAT ARE YOUR LOW POINTS OF THE WEEK AS A COUPLE?

WHAT IS THE ONE THING YOU WANT THE OTHER PERSON TO WORK ON THIS COMING WEEK?

WHAT IMPORTANT EVENTS, MEETINGS, OR OBLIGATIONS DO YOU HAVE THIS WEEK?

FOLLOW UP:

DID YOU WORK ON THE ISSUES THAT WERE ADDRESSED LAST WEEK?

WEEKLY RELATIONSHIP MEETING

WEEK OF ....

BOTH OF YOU TAKE TURNS TELLING EACH OTHER SOMETHING POSITIVE ABOUT ONE ANOTHER:

HOW ARE YOU DOING AS INDIVIDUALS? IS SOMETHING WEIGHING ON YOU OUTSIDE OF YOUR HOME?

WHAT ARE YOUR HIGH POINTS OF THE WEEK AS A COUPLE?

WHAT ARE YOUR LOW POINTS OF THE WEEK AS A COUPLE?

WHAT IS THE ONE THING YOU WANT THE OTHER PERSON TO WORK ON THIS COMING WEEK?

WHAT IMPORTANT EVENTS, MEETINGS, OR OBLIGATIONS DO YOU HAVE THIS WEEK?

FOLLOW UP:

DID YOU WORK ON THE ISSUES THAT WERE ADDRESSED LAST WEEK?

Let's talk about it!

MONTH 9

IF YOU ARE IN A BAD MOOD, DO YOU PREFER TO BE LEFT ALONE OR HAVE SOMEONE CHEER YOU UP?

MONTH 9 CHALLENGE

It's time to have some real out of the box fun! This month's challenge is a

"Thrift Store Challenge"

This challenge is a ton of fun and for sure something to get you out of your normal routine! It can also double as an extra date night this month. What you need to do is simple!

Go online and find a new restaurant in town (make reservations if you need to and don't be late!)

Visit your local thrift shop or Goodwill

You each have $20 and 30 minutes to find a complete outfit (top, bottoms, and shoes) for the other person

Get dressed in the dressing room and wear your "new" clothes out to dinner (Well, after you pay of course)

Go out and have an amazing night filled with laughs and great food

Be sure to take tons of pictures and share them on social media using the hashtag #justelopethriftchallenge

Intimacy TRACKER

DOCUMENT YOUR DAILY AFFECTIONS FOR EACH OTHER

MONTH..........

SUNDAY	MONDAY	TUESDAY	WEDNESDAY	THURSDAY	FRIDAY	SATURDAY

WEEKLY RELATIONSHIP MEETING

WEEK OF ....

BOTH OF YOU TAKE TURNS TELLING EACH OTHER SOMETHING POSITIVE ABOUT ONE ANOTHER:

HOW ARE YOU DOING AS INDIVIDUALS? IS SOMETHING WEIGHING ON YOU OUTSIDE OF YOUR HOME?

WHAT ARE YOUR HIGH POINTS OF THE WEEK AS A COUPLE?

WHAT ARE YOUR LOW POINTS OF THE WEEK AS A COUPLE?

WHAT IS THE ONE THING YOU WANT THE OTHER PERSON TO WORK ON THIS COMING WEEK?

WHAT IMPORTANT EVENTS, MEETINGS, OR OBLIGATIONS DO YOU HAVE THIS WEEK?

FOLLOW UP:

DID YOU WORK ON THE ISSUES THAT WERE ADDRESSED LAST WEEK?

WEEKLY RELATIONSHIP MEETING

WEEK OF ....

BOTH OF YOU TAKE TURNS TELLING EACH OTHER SOMETHING POSITIVE ABOUT ONE ANOTHER:

HOW ARE YOU DOING AS INDIVIDUALS? IS SOMETHING WEIGHING ON YOU OUTSIDE OF YOUR HOME?

WHAT ARE YOUR HIGH POINTS OF THE WEEK AS A COUPLE?

WHAT ARE YOUR LOW POINTS OF THE WEEK AS A COUPLE?

WHAT IS THE ONE THING YOU WANT THE OTHER PERSON TO WORK ON THIS COMING WEEK?

WHAT IMPORTANT EVENTS, MEETINGS, OR OBLIGATIONS DO YOU HAVE THIS WEEK?

FOLLOW UP:

DID YOU WORK ON THE ISSUES THAT WERE ADDRESSED LAST WEEK?

WEEKLY RELATIONSHIP MEETING

WEEK OF ....

BOTH OF YOU TAKE TURNS TELLING EACH OTHER SOMETHING POSITIVE ABOUT ONE ANOTHER:

HOW ARE YOU DOING AS INDIVIDUALS? IS SOMETHING WEIGHING ON YOU OUTSIDE OF YOUR HOME?

WHAT ARE YOUR HIGH POINTS OF THE WEEK AS A COUPLE?

WHAT ARE YOUR LOW POINTS OF THE WEEK AS A COUPLE?

WHAT IS THE ONE THING YOU WANT THE OTHER PERSON TO WORK ON THIS COMING WEEK?

WHAT IMPORTANT EVENTS, MEETINGS, OR OBLIGATIONS DO YOU HAVE THIS WEEK?

FOLLOW UP:

DID YOU WORK ON THE ISSUES THAT WERE ADDRESSED LAST WEEK?

WEEKLY RELATIONSHIP MEETING

WEEK OF ....

BOTH OF YOU TAKE TURNS TELLING EACH OTHER SOMETHING POSITIVE ABOUT ONE ANOTHER:

HOW ARE YOU DOING AS INDIVIDUALS? IS SOMETHING WEIGHING ON YOU OUTSIDE OF YOUR HOME?

WHAT ARE YOUR HIGH POINTS OF THE WEEK AS A COUPLE?

WHAT ARE YOUR LOW POINTS OF THE WEEK AS A COUPLE?

WHAT IS THE ONE THING YOU WANT THE OTHER PERSON TO WORK ON THIS COMING WEEK?

WHAT IMPORTANT EVENTS, MEETINGS, OR OBLIGATIONS DO YOU HAVE THIS WEEK?

FOLLOW UP:

DID YOU WORK ON THE ISSUES THAT WERE ADDRESSED LAST WEEK?

Let's talk about it!

MONTH 10

IF OUR LOVE WAS NOVEL WHAT WOULD THE TITLE BE?

COUPLE'S INTERVIEW:

HOW DID YOU MEET?

HOW LONG DID YOU DATE BEFORE YOU KNEW THIS WAS THE PERSON YOU WANT TO SPEND THE REST OF YOUR LIFE WITH?

WHAT WAS IT ABOUT THE OTHER PERSON THAT MADE THEM DIFFERENT FROM ANYONE ELSE YOU HAD EVER BEEN WITH?

HOW DO YOU "FIGHT" FAIR?

DO YOU BELIEVE IN GENDER ROLES WHEN IT COMES TO CHORES IN YOUR HOUSEHOLD?

WHAT DO YOU THINK THE MOST CHALLENGING PART ABOUT BEING MARRIED/IN A COMMITTED RELATIONSHIP IS?

COUPLE'S INTERVIEW:

WHAT IS THE BEST ADVICE YOU RECEIVED THAT HELPED YOU THROUGH ROUGH TIMES OR HELPED YOU PREVENT ROUGH TIMES?

DO YOU "LIKE" EACH OTHER EVERY DAY?

DO YOU EVER FEEL BORED WITH YOUR RELATIONSHIP? IF SO, WHAT STEPS DO YOU TAKE TO SPICE THINGS UP?

DO YOU GET ALONG WITH YOUR IN-LAWS? IF NOT, HOW DOES THAT EFFECT YOUR MARRIAGE/RELATIONSHIP?

WHO HANDLES THE FINANCES AND WHY?

COMPLETE THIS SENTENCE: THE BEST PART OF OUR LIFE TOGETHER IS.......

Intimacy TRACKER

DOCUMENT YOUR DAILY AFFECTIONS FOR EACH OTHER

MONTH ....

SUNDAY	MONDAY	TUESDAY	WEDNESDAY	THURSDAY	FRIDAY	SATURDAY

WEEKLY RELATIONSHIP MEETING

WEEK OF ....

BOTH OF YOU TAKE TURNS TELLING EACH OTHER SOMETHING POSITIVE ABOUT ONE ANOTHER:

HOW ARE YOU DOING AS INDIVIDUALS? IS SOMETHING WEIGHING ON YOU OUTSIDE OF YOUR HOME?

WHAT ARE YOUR HIGH POINTS OF THE WEEK AS A COUPLE?

WHAT ARE YOUR LOW POINTS OF THE WEEK AS A COUPLE?

WHAT IS THE ONE THING YOU WANT THE OTHER PERSON TO WORK ON THIS COMING WEEK?

WHAT IMPORTANT EVENTS, MEETINGS, OR OBLIGATIONS DO YOU HAVE THIS WEEK?

FOLLOW UP:

DID YOU WORK ON THE ISSUES THAT WERE ADDRESSED LAST WEEK?

WEEKLY RELATIONSHIP MEETING

WEEK OF ....

BOTH OF YOU TAKE TURNS TELLING EACH OTHER SOMETHING POSITIVE ABOUT ONE ANOTHER:

HOW ARE YOU DOING AS INDIVIDUALS? IS SOMETHING WEIGHING ON YOU OUTSIDE OF YOUR HOME?

WHAT ARE YOUR HIGH POINTS OF THE WEEK AS A COUPLE?

WHAT ARE YOUR LOW POINTS OF THE WEEK AS A COUPLE?

WHAT IS THE ONE THING YOU WANT THE OTHER PERSON TO WORK ON THIS COMING WEEK?

WHAT IMPORTANT EVENTS, MEETINGS, OR OBLIGATIONS DO YOU HAVE THIS WEEK?

FOLLOW UP:

DID YOU WORK ON THE ISSUES THAT WERE ADDRESSED LAST WEEK?

WEEKLY RELATIONSHIP MEETING

WEEK OF ....

BOTH OF YOU TAKE TURNS TELLING EACH OTHER SOMETHING POSITIVE ABOUT ONE ANOTHER:

HOW ARE YOU DOING AS INDIVIDUALS? IS SOMETHING WEIGHING ON YOU OUTSIDE OF YOUR HOME?

WHAT ARE YOUR HIGH POINTS OF THE WEEK AS A COUPLE?

WHAT ARE YOUR LOW POINTS OF THE WEEK AS A COUPLE?

WHAT IS THE ONE THING YOU WANT THE OTHER PERSON TO WORK ON THIS COMING WEEK?

WHAT IMPORTANT EVENTS, MEETINGS, OR OBLIGATIONS DO YOU HAVE THIS WEEK?

FOLLOW UP:

DID YOU WORK ON THE ISSUES THAT WERE ADDRESSED LAST WEEK?

WEEKLY RELATIONSHIP MEETING

WEEK OF ....

BOTH OF YOU TAKE TURNS TELLING EACH OTHER SOMETHING POSITIVE ABOUT ONE ANOTHER:

HOW ARE YOU DOING AS INDIVIDUALS? IS SOMETHING WEIGHING ON YOU OUTSIDE OF YOUR HOME?

WHAT ARE YOUR HIGH POINTS OF THE WEEK AS A COUPLE?

WHAT ARE YOUR LOW POINTS OF THE WEEK AS A COUPLE?

WHAT IS THE ONE THING YOU WANT THE OTHER PERSON TO WORK ON THIS COMING WEEK?

WHAT IMPORTANT EVENTS, MEETINGS, OR OBLIGATIONS DO YOU HAVE THIS WEEK?

FOLLOW UP:

DID YOU WORK ON THE ISSUES THAT WERE ADDRESSED LAST WEEK?

Let's talk about it!

....
....
....
....
....
....
....
....
....
....
....
....
....
....
....
....
....

MONTH 11

CAN YOU REMEMBER A TIME IN YOUR LIFE YOU FELT THE MOST ALIVE? TELL ME EVERYTHING ABOUT THAT MEMORY.

MONTH 11 CHALLENGE

Congratulations! You have made it to month 11 of our #RelationshipGoals journal. Hopefully through all of the challenges and weekly meetings you have learned that in order to be #Goals it takes some serious work from the both of you as individuals and as a couple.

Your final challenge is to come up with 10 reasons why your love story is #RelationshipGoals. When times get hard or you feel a strain on your relationship look back to these reasons as a reminder of how much you have grown as a couple and just how deep your love is for one another.

REASONS WE ARE:
#RELATIONSHIP GOALS

....

....

....

....

....

....

....

....

....

....

Intimacy TRACKER

DOCUMENT YOUR DAILY AFFECTIONS FOR EACH OTHER

MONTH..........

SUNDAY	MONDAY	TUESDAY	WEDNESDAY	THURSDAY	FRIDAY	SATURDAY

WEEKLY RELATIONSHIP MEETING

WEEK OF ....

BOTH OF YOU TAKE TURNS TELLING EACH OTHER SOMETHING POSITIVE ABOUT ONE ANOTHER:

HOW ARE YOU DOING AS INDIVIDUALS? IS SOMETHING WEIGHING ON YOU OUTSIDE OF YOUR HOME?

WHAT ARE YOUR HIGH POINTS OF THE WEEK AS A COUPLE?

WHAT ARE YOUR LOW POINTS OF THE WEEK AS A COUPLE?

WHAT IS THE ONE THING YOU WANT THE OTHER PERSON TO WORK ON THIS COMING WEEK?

WHAT IMPORTANT EVENTS, MEETINGS, OR OBLIGATIONS DO YOU HAVE THIS WEEK?

FOLLOW UP:

DID YOU WORK ON THE ISSUES THAT WERE ADDRESSED LAST WEEK?

WEEKLY RELATIONSHIP MEETING

WEEK OF ....

BOTH OF YOU TAKE TURNS TELLING EACH OTHER SOMETHING POSITIVE ABOUT ONE ANOTHER:

HOW ARE YOU DOING AS INDIVIDUALS? IS SOMETHING WEIGHING ON YOU OUTSIDE OF YOUR HOME?

WHAT ARE YOUR HIGH POINTS OF THE WEEK AS A COUPLE?

WHAT ARE YOUR LOW POINTS OF THE WEEK AS A COUPLE?

WHAT IS THE ONE THING YOU WANT THE OTHER PERSON TO WORK ON THIS COMING WEEK?

WHAT IMPORTANT EVENTS, MEETINGS, OR OBLIGATIONS DO YOU HAVE THIS WEEK?

FOLLOW UP:

DID YOU WORK ON THE ISSUES THAT WERE ADDRESSED LAST WEEK?

WEEKLY RELATIONSHIP MEETING

WEEK OF ....

BOTH OF YOU TAKE TURNS TELLING EACH OTHER SOMETHING POSITIVE ABOUT ONE ANOTHER:

HOW ARE YOU DOING AS INDIVIDUALS? IS SOMETHING WEIGHING ON YOU OUTSIDE OF YOUR HOME?

WHAT ARE YOUR HIGH POINTS OF THE WEEK AS A COUPLE?

WHAT ARE YOUR LOW POINTS OF THE WEEK AS A COUPLE?

WHAT IS THE ONE THING YOU WANT THE OTHER PERSON TO WORK ON THIS COMING WEEK?

WHAT IMPORTANT EVENTS, MEETINGS, OR OBLIGATIONS DO YOU HAVE THIS WEEK?

FOLLOW UP:

DID YOU WORK ON THE ISSUES THAT WERE ADDRESSED LAST WEEK?

WEEKLY RELATIONSHIP MEETING

WEEK OF ....

BOTH OF YOU TAKE TURNS TELLING EACH OTHER SOMETHING POSITIVE ABOUT ONE ANOTHER:

HOW ARE YOU DOING AS INDIVIDUALS? IS SOMETHING WEIGHING ON YOU OUTSIDE OF YOUR HOME?

WHAT ARE YOUR HIGH POINTS OF THE WEEK AS A COUPLE?

WHAT ARE YOUR LOW POINTS OF THE WEEK AS A COUPLE?

WHAT IS THE ONE THING YOU WANT THE OTHER PERSON TO WORK ON THIS COMING WEEK?

WHAT IMPORTANT EVENTS, MEETINGS, OR OBLIGATIONS DO YOU HAVE THIS WEEK?

FOLLOW UP:

DID YOU WORK ON THE ISSUES THAT WERE ADDRESSED LAST WEEK?

Let's talk about it!

MONTH 12

WHAT WOULD YOU WANT YOUR LEGACY TO BE?

COUPLE'S INTERVIEW:

HOW DID YOU MEET?

HOW LONG DID YOU DATE BEFORE YOU KNEW THIS WAS THE PERSON YOU WANT TO SPEND THE REST OF YOUR LIFE WITH?

WHAT WAS IT ABOUT THE OTHER PERSON THAT MADE THEM DIFFERENT FROM ANYONE ELSE YOU HAD EVER BEEN WITH?

HOW DO YOU "FIGHT" FAIR?

DO YOU BELIEVE IN GENDER ROLES WHEN IT COMES TO CHORES IN YOUR HOUSEHOLD?

WHAT DO YOU THINK THE MOST CHALLENGING PART ABOUT BEING MARRIED/IN A COMMITTED RELATIONSHIP IS?

COUPLE'S INTERVIEW:

WHAT IS THE BEST ADVICE YOU RECEIVED THAT HELPED YOU THROUGH ROUGH TIMES OR HELPED YOU PREVENT ROUGH TIMES?

DO YOU "LIKE" EACH OTHER EVERY DAY?

DO YOU EVER FEEL BORED WITH YOUR RELATIONSHIP? IF SO, WHAT STEPS DO YOU TAKE TO SPICE THINGS UP?

DO YOU GET ALONG WITH YOUR IN-LAWS? IF NOT, HOW DOES THAT EFFECT YOUR MARRIAGE/RELATIONSHIP?

WHO HANDLES THE FINANCES AND WHY?

COMPLETE THIS SENTENCE: THE BEST PART OF OUR LIFE TOGETHER IS.......

Intimacy TRACKER
DOCUMENT YOUR DAILY AFFECTIONS FOR EACH OTHER

MONTH ....

SUNDAY	MONDAY	TUESDAY	WEDNESDAY	THURSDAY	FRIDAY	SATURDAY

WEEKLY RELATIONSHIP MEETING

WEEK OF ....

BOTH OF YOU TAKE TURNS TELLING EACH OTHER SOMETHING POSITIVE ABOUT ONE ANOTHER:

HOW ARE YOU DOING AS INDIVIDUALS? IS SOMETHING WEIGHING ON YOU OUTSIDE OF YOUR HOME?

WHAT ARE YOUR HIGH POINTS OF THE WEEK AS A COUPLE?

WHAT ARE YOUR LOW POINTS OF THE WEEK AS A COUPLE?

WHAT IS THE ONE THING YOU WANT THE OTHER PERSON TO WORK ON THIS COMING WEEK?

WHAT IMPORTANT EVENTS, MEETINGS, OR OBLIGATIONS DO YOU HAVE THIS WEEK?

FOLLOW UP:

DID YOU WORK ON THE ISSUES THAT WERE ADDRESSED LAST WEEK?

WEEKLY RELATIONSHIP MEETING

WEEK OF ....

BOTH OF YOU TAKE TURNS TELLING EACH OTHER SOMETHING POSITIVE ABOUT ONE ANOTHER:

HOW ARE YOU DOING AS INDIVIDUALS? IS SOMETHING WEIGHING ON YOU OUTSIDE OF YOUR HOME?

WHAT ARE YOUR HIGH POINTS OF THE WEEK AS A COUPLE?

WHAT ARE YOUR LOW POINTS OF THE WEEK AS A COUPLE?

WHAT IS THE ONE THING YOU WANT THE OTHER PERSON TO WORK ON THIS COMING WEEK?

WHAT IMPORTANT EVENTS, MEETINGS, OR OBLIGATIONS DO YOU HAVE THIS WEEK?

FOLLOW UP:

DID YOU WORK ON THE ISSUES THAT WERE ADDRESSED LAST WEEK?

WEEKLY RELATIONSHIP MEETING

WEEK OF ....

BOTH OF YOU TAKE TURNS TELLING EACH OTHER SOMETHING POSITIVE ABOUT ONE ANOTHER:

HOW ARE YOU DOING AS INDIVIDUALS? IS SOMETHING WEIGHING ON YOU OUTSIDE OF YOUR HOME?

WHAT ARE YOUR HIGH POINTS OF THE WEEK AS A COUPLE?

WHAT ARE YOUR LOW POINTS OF THE WEEK AS A COUPLE?

WHAT IS THE ONE THING YOU WANT THE OTHER PERSON TO WORK ON THIS COMING WEEK?

WHAT IMPORTANT EVENTS, MEETINGS, OR OBLIGATIONS DO YOU HAVE THIS WEEK?

FOLLOW UP:

DID YOU WORK ON THE ISSUES THAT WERE ADDRESSED LAST WEEK?

WEEKLY RELATIONSHIP MEETING

WEEK OF ....

BOTH OF YOU TAKE TURNS TELLING EACH OTHER SOMETHING POSITIVE ABOUT ONE ANOTHER:

HOW ARE YOU DOING AS INDIVIDUALS? IS SOMETHING WEIGHING ON YOU OUTSIDE OF YOUR HOME?

WHAT ARE YOUR HIGH POINTS OF THE WEEK AS A COUPLE?

WHAT ARE YOUR LOW POINTS OF THE WEEK AS A COUPLE?

WHAT IS THE ONE THING YOU WANT THE OTHER PERSON TO WORK ON THIS COMING WEEK?

WHAT IMPORTANT EVENTS, MEETINGS, OR OBLIGATIONS DO YOU HAVE THIS WEEK?

FOLLOW UP:

DID YOU WORK ON THE ISSUES THAT WERE ADDRESSED LAST WEEK?

Let's talk about it!

....
....
....
....
....
....
....
....
....
....
....
....
....
....
....
....
....

VISIT US ONLINE AT WWW.JUSTELOPE.NET FOR MORE MONTHLY CHALLENGES, PRINTABLES AND TIPS TO GROW YOUR RELATIONSHIP.

xoxo,

Jennifer Allen

Made in the USA
Columbia, SC
12 September 2019